Family Roller Coaster

RIDING THE HIGHS AND LOWS
OF EMOTIONS... TOGETHER

by Dr. Randy T. Johnson

with contributions by:

Noble Baird	John Hubbard
John Carter	Debbie Kerr
Trevor Cole	Josh Lahring
Caleb Combs	Chuck Lindsey
Carole Combs	Wes McCullough
Isaiah Combs	Philip Piasecki
Jayson Combs	John Sanchez
Jim Combs	Ryan Story
Josh Combs	Roy Townsend
Bryan Fox	Kim Vallance
Donna Fox	Mike Vallance
Michael Fox	Kyle Wendel
Debbie Gabarra	Katrina Young
Matt Hatton	

Copyright © 2017 The River Church

All rights reserved. No part of this book may be reproduced or transmitted in any form or by any means, electronic or mechanical, including photocopying, recording or by any information storage and retrieval system, without the written permission of The River Church. Inquiries should be sent to the publisher.

First Edition, January 2017

Published by:
The River Church
8393 E. Holly Rd.
Holly, MI 48442

Scriptures are taken from the Bible,
English Standard Version (ESV)

THE RIVER CHURCH

Printed in the United States of America

CONTENTS

WEEK 1: ANGER
07 Study Guide
13 Devotion 1: Self-Control
15 Devotion 2: Brotherly Shove
17 Devotion 3: We are all Teachers of Something
19 Devotion 4: Two Ears, One Mouth
21 Devotion 5: The Anger Inside
23 Devotion 6: The Daer

WEEK 2: LUST
27 Study Guide
33 Devotion 1: Eye "Sour" Candy
35 Devotion 2: The Conversation
37 Devotion 3: Keep Your Eyes to Yourself
39 Devotion 4: Clear the Stage
41 Devotion 5: Desires of the Heart
43 Devotion 6: Dear Me

WEEK 3: PROMISES
47 Study Guide
53 Devotion 1: Standing on the Promises
55 Devotion 2: Word
57 Devotion 3: Only Yes or No
59 Devotion 4: He Keeps His Promises
61 Devotion 5: We'll Go Tomorrow, I Promise
63 Devotion 6: Higher Standards

WEEK 4: RETALIATION
67 Study Guide
77 Devotion 1: Don't Retaliate, Bless
79 Devotion 2: I for an Eye
81 Devotion 3: Silent Retaliation
83 Devotion 4: How do We Respond
85 Devotion 5: The Potential Prisoner
87 Devotion 6: The Will or Thy Will

APPENDIX 1: DIVORCE?
93 What does the Bible Say?

APPENDIX 2: WORKSHOP NOTES
105 Money
111 Intimacy in Marriage
113 Conflict Resolution
117 Grand Parenting
119 Raising Teens
121 Addiction in the Family
123 The 7 C's of Parenting Preschoolers
125 Venus, Mars, and My Kids are Chasing Pluto
129 Blended to Mended
131 Shepherding our Kids
133 Effective Discipline in a Defective World
137 Single Parenting

1

ANGER
Pastor Trevor Cole | Operations Pastor

It is a scary scene when something like a train goes barreling out of control. Most things out of control are scary. It may not always seem frightening, but uncontrolled anger has devastating effects on everyone around it. The word "family" means so much more than the people we are physically related to; it inherently carries the idea of relationships. Those relationships are fragile and can be eaten away at by years of uncontrolled anger or ripped apart in a moment of rage. Take a moment and think about how uncontrolled anger has impacted your own life and the lives of others you know.

As we begin this study, I want you to avoid placing yourself on some kind of anger scale or trying to justify your anger in any way. All of us get angry at times. We may not all handle it in the same way, and it may be more noticeable for some than others, but we all deal with it in some way.

Learning how to control our anger has multiple parts, but where does anger begin? _____
_____
_____
_____

I love the way that Proverbs 4:23 says it. *"Keep your heart with all vigilance, for from it flow the springs of life."*

What do you think he means by saying, "Keep your heart with all vigilance?" _____
_____
_____
_____

Ephesians 5:15-20:
"Be very careful, then, how you live—not as unwise but as wise, 16 making the most of every opportunity, because the days are evil. 17 Therefore do not be foolish, but understand what the Lord's will is. 18 Do not get drunk on wine, which leads to debauchery. Instead, be filled with the Spirit, 19 speaking to one another with psalms, hymns, and songs from the Spirit. Sing and make music from your heart to the Lord, 20 always giving thanks to God the Father for everything, in the name of our Lord Jesus Christ."

The above passage reminds us that we need to be filled with the Spirit and not controlled by drunkenness. How is that similar to being controlled by anger? _____
_____
_____
_____

God longs for us to be guided by Him. When we allow anger to take over, it takes God out of the equation, and we give in to the impulses and whims of our emotions. In a moment of anger, we will often say or do things we would never normally do.

What are some scenarios in your daily life where you are most tempted to lose your cool? _____
_____
_____

If we can learn to give God control of our emotions, then we are on our way to controlling our anger. We must also ask ourselves some questions about how we handle some of the situations that cause our anger. Almost everyone deals with their frustrations in one of two ways:

1. Blow Up - When someone says something you disagree with or do not like, or circumstances just do not go your way, you explode at anyone nearby and often those with the closest relationships to you. Again, do not put yourself on some scale here. Not everyone who blows up does so at maximum volume. It may come across as a snarky response or joke meant, but it is really meant to hurt the other person.

2. Clam Up - This way of handling frustration seems much more "spiritual" on the surface. The problems begin to show up over time when you develop resentment after days, weeks, or years of small frustrations. This may seem like you are controlling your anger, but you are just burying it, only for it to rise to the surface again later on.

These are two opposite ends of the spectrum so most people will be somewhere in the middle, but we all lean towards one or the other. Which category would you place yourself in? _____
_____
_____

Take a moment and write down a few times in your recent past where you handled your frustrations by blowing up or clamming up. _____

_____

_____

_____

Proverbs 15:1 says, **"A soft answer turns away wrath, but a harsh word stirs up anger."** It doesn't say a "loud" answer, but a "harsh" answer." In the moments you feel like exploding at someone or just hiding the frustration down deep, ask God for the right attitude. Anger, and how we handle it, begins in the heart. We have to learn to give God control of our heart so that anger does not. However, like most things God has given us, anger has its place.

Ephesians 4:26 reads: **"Be angry and do not sin; do not let the sun go down on your anger."** Give some examples of things we should be angry at. _____

_____

_____

_____

John 2:13-18: **"The Passover of the Jews was at hand, and Jesus went up to Jerusalem. 14 In the temple he found those who were selling oxen and sheep and pigeons, and the money-changers sitting there. 15 And making a whip of cords, he drove them all out of the temple, with the sheep and oxen. And he poured out the coins of the money-changers and overturned their tables. 16 And he told those who sold the pigeons, "Take these things away; do not make my Father's house a house of trade."**

Jesus got angry at the disrespect shown at the temple. We should get angry at sin that tries to control our lives and the lives of others. Anger at the right things can create a God-given energy to solve problems. As followers of Jesus, we should be a force for good in this world.

What types of victims in the world could benefit from the problem solving energy of anger? _____
_____
_____

How can you be a part of the solution? _____
_____
_____

How do you want to influence your family? Do you want them to remember the moments where your anger got the best of you? Do you want them to learn, from you, the proper way to respond to the countless difficult situations they will face in life? Do not let anger control you. Learn to let God guide your heart and emotions, to not take things personally, to attack the problem, not a person. Only then can we begin to lead our families in the way God has called us to.

ANGER: DEVOTION 1

SELF-CONTROL

Michael Fox | Production Director

I have had many instances in my life where I have become angry with someone. For various reasons, they did not follow through with something they said that they would, they did not communicate well with me, or they said hurtful words to me. What I have found more often than not is that once I sit down with that person and talk to them about it, I often misunderstood the situation and the conflict was not nearly what I made it out to be. Typically, selfishness on my part contributes to a large part of my anger. What I have also found is when I have chosen not to talk with the person right away about it, I become very bitter and angrier as the days and weeks go on. This ends up elevating the situation, as well as interfering with my relationship with God. In Galatians 5:22-23, we see characteristics of the Holy Spirit in our daily activities:

Galatians 5:22-23
But the fruit of the Spirit is love, joy, peace, patience, kindness, goodness, faithfulness, gentleness, self-control; against such things there is no law.

Seeking God for self-control is a key part of overcoming anger in our daily lives.

Recently, we have been dealing with anger with our six-year-old son when he does not get his way. I have noticed a few valuable things here. If we, as his parents, respond to his anger with anger it usually only causes more anger from him. However, if we deal with his anger promptly and calmly, the issue is always resolved quickly, and he is beginning to learn more self-control and repentance.

Ephesians 4:26-27
Be angry and do not sin; do not let the sun go down on your anger, and give no opportunity to the devil.

There are two key points that I pull from Ephesians 4:26-27. First, **"Be angry and do not sin."** In life, anger is sometimes inevitable, and there are instances where anger is going to happen. However, consider the **"do not sin"** portion of this Scripture. Remember that our anger does not produce the righteousness of God (James 1:20).

James 1:19-20
Know this, my beloved brothers: let every person be quick to hear, slow to speak, slow to anger; for the anger of man does not produce the righteousness of God.

Secondly, "do not let the sun go down on your anger." What I get from this portion of Scripture is a time limit of sorts. Deal with anger right away, and remember God's grace and forgiveness.

Mark 11:25
"And whenever you stand praying, forgive, if you have anything against anyone, so that your Father also who is in heaven may forgive you your trespasses."

ANGER: DEVOTION 2

BROTHERLY SHOVE

Philip Piasecki | Worship Leader

My brother and I have always been very competitive with each other. We grew up playing all kinds of sports against each other, and it always seemed to end up with one of us angry with the other one. I would beat him at one on one in basketball and he would chase me around the yard trying his hardest to throw the basketball at me and blast me in the head. I remember one time we were playing football with my parents in the front yard and my brother scored a touchdown. He decided to taunt me after scoring by repeatedly saying, "Nah nah you can't touch this." I had finally had enough and tackled him as hard as I could. After hours of tears and a hospital visit for him, it was discovered I had broken his collarbone. I had let my anger get the best of me, and there were severe consequences. Still to this day, I feel guilty that I lashed out in the way I did.

When we think of anger, most people think of a physical outburst like the one I had about my brother. However, physical outbursts like that point towards more troubling issues within one's heart. Ephesians 4:31-32 says, *"Let all bitterness, and wrath, and anger, and clamour, and evil speaking, be put away from you, with all malice: and be ye kind one to another, tenderhearted, forgiving one another, even as God for Christ's sake hath forgiven you."* In this Scripture, we are instructed to put away our anger and to be kind to one another. Most of the time I am a very patient person, but there are seasons in my life when I find myself getting angry much easier. This is when I need to stop and reflect on how I have been living my life. I often find that the answer to my anger is that I have not been spending enough time with Christ. I am sure many people feel the same way. Sometimes they can control their anger, and other times they feel like they get angry at everything. To put away anger successfully and all those things from Ephesians 4:31-32, we constantly need to be focused on what Christ did for us.

Sin makes God angry, and instead of pouring out His anger and wrath on us, He poured it out on His Son. When the truth of what Christ did for us is at the forefront of our lives, we will find ourselves much less likely to get angry. My desire is to forgive people just as Christ forgave me and not get mad at them for silly things. As believers, we should reflect the love of Christ to one another and not constantly be angry with each other. If you struggle with anger, pray that God would deliver you from that. Focus on the amazing things that Christ has done for you. Let's be a Church that puts away anger, and reflects the holiness of Christ to a broken world.

ANGER: DEVOTION 3

WE ARE ALL TEACHERS OF SOMETHING

Pastor Ryan Story | Student Pastor

Ever since my son was born, there has been one thing I have taught him that my wife never liked. If I say the word "head-butt" and put my head down, my son will get a huge smile on and come give me a baby head-butt. He laughs and then goes back and plays. One day I got a text from my wife that started with "Broly is your son." Instantly I knew I was in trouble. She proceeded to tell me that when she asked him for a kiss, he gave her a head-butt. Instantly all of "I've been watching you" by Rodney Atkins started playing in my head.

Proverbs 22:6 says, ***"Train up a child in the way he should go"*** In this situation, I am not too worried about Broly walking around becoming a menace to society by head-butting random people. However, I started thinking, "what are some other actions that I am inadvertently training my son to do that I do not want him to learn?" I have been working with children and teens, in ministry and schools, for close to ten years now. One thing that has always stuck out to me is how much children learn from their parents. If a parent is affectionate, then the child is usually affectionate. If a parent is shy, then the child is sometimes shy. If the parent is playful, then the child generally is playful. Now the sad truth that I have seen is, if a parent gets angry often, the child displays the same tendencies. It is amazing to think how much influence parents have.

The reality of life is we all have anger problems. If we go by the definition of anger, it would be "a strong feeling of annoyance, displeasure, or hostility." I think when people hear the word anger they instantly think rage, yelling, throwing things, and etcetera. I feel there are quite a few people who have "anger issues," but they display them in a quiet way. Let us be honest; you have been in a situation where you were completely annoyed, but you had a smile on your face. In the family, anger can become something that destroys everything. Sadly, when I look at the exact definition of anger, I realized that some of my bad habits came from my parents and I am terrified to pass those on to my son. Take a second to think of the ways that you deal with things that annoy you, things that displease you, and things that cause you to becoming hostel. Now look at your children, do they display the same tendencies? How are you training up your child to handle anger? It is amazing to think how much you can teach about Jesus just on how you respond to a stressful situation.

ANGER: DEVOTION 4

TWO EARS, ONE MOUTH

Donna Fox | Assistant to the Growth Pastor

"My dear brothers and sisters, take note of this: Everyone should be quick to listen, slow to speak and slow to become angry, because human anger does not produce the righteousness that God desires." James 1:19-20

When I was younger, I used to talk a lot. If I were telling someone something that happened, I would go into every detail and go on and on so that I was sure he or she knew everything. They would grow weary of my story and finally say, "Just get to the point!" If they were trying to tell me something, I would likely interrupt with my take on the situation or a similar story that happened to me. I was not good at listening.

As I have matured, I have tried more and more to heed the advice of James **"quick to listen, slow to speak and slow to become angry."** We have two ears and one mouth. It seems like God designed us that way for a reason! Listen twice as much as you talk.

If you are in a situation where you become angry, the first thing you need to do is take a step back, take a deep breath, calm down, and LISTEN. Do not talk. In your anger, you will likely get madder and madder as the words come out of your mouth. Calmly listen to the other person's point of view with your two ears, then calmly talk with your one mouth. Listen twice as much as you talk.

It has taken me a long time to learn this lesson, and it has not been easy, especially with family. With our families, we are the most comfortable. We have a history there. With strangers, we are more guarded. I have a hard time keeping my mouth shut sometimes, especially with those closest to me, but when I have, I know that it has saved me a lot of heartache and anger. After I listen, calm down, and look objectively at the situation, it never seems as bad as I originally thought. Time calms the anger.

Maybe your anger does not subside. Maybe your anger just grows and grows into bitterness or rage. Is that glorifying God? When people look at you, do they see Jesus? Do they see love, joy, peace? Do they see anger? 1 Corinthians 10:31 says, ***"So, whether you eat or drink, or whatever you do, do all to the glory of God."***

God calls us to edify one another, be encouraging, and loving. 1 Thessalonians 5:11says, ***"Therefore encourage one another and build each other up, just as in fact you are doing."*** We are not pleasing God by being angry. The bitterness in our hearts and the words coming out of our mouths are surely not what God desires.

So step back, take a minute to pray, and let the anger subside before you speak. Maybe the situation will resolve itself and you will not have to speak at all!

ANGER: DEVOTION 5

THE ANGER INSIDE

Bryan Fox | Deacon of Facilities

When I get angry, I tend to keep my anger inside of me. I had a good example of this happen a while back. I spent over a day thinking about unfair it was for the other person to say what was said, how I was right, he was wrong, how I should handle the eventual conversation which I knew had to happen along with a lot of different scenarios of that conversation playing out in my head. A simple conversation the next day cleared up the issue with my complete understanding of why the other person acted the way he did; however, I spent way too much time and energy on something that in the end was quite simple.

I once saw a picture that had two people facing each other and between them was a number on the ground. As each person looked at the number, one saw a six and the other saw a nine. Now either person could argue all day long that they were right with the number they saw and conversely that the other person was wrong. This kind of situation can be the basis of anger in many daily events. I know that I am right based on the factual information that I see, which means that you then must be wrong. Obviously, there are always two sides to every story. Even when you are certain you are right, you need to understand the other person's perspective so both sides know what the real issue is.

In the end, what does anger really get you? If you waste time pondering about what might be, instead of confronting the issue, it takes away from what God wants us to do. Paul wrote in Philippians 4:8, *"Finally, brothers, whatever is true, whatever is honorable, whatever is just, whatever is pure, whatever is lovely, whatever is commendable, if there is*

any excellence, if there is anything worthy of praise, think about these things."

Please take some time and read what the Bible says about anger. Some verses I picked are as follows:

Ephesians 4:26-27
Proverbs 15:18; 19:11; 30:33
Colossians 3:8-13

Remember when you become angry, deal with it quickly, delicately, and above all else, Biblically!

ANGER: DEVOTION 6

THE DAER

Noble Baird | Guest Services Director

When I was a child, I remember being sent to my room for my tendency to be disobedient to my parents. One day, when my father sent me to my room, I was especially unhappy with him. I slammed the door, grabbed a pen and paper, and wrote a note to my parents to tape to the outside of my door. At the top of the page, I drew a hangman stick figure with the words, "You can came in if you daer" written underneath it. Yes, in my frustration and anger, I spelled the words "come" and "dare" wrong, which made it even funnier for my parents. However, I was able to convey through my message on the door, the anger I had towards my parents for punishing me.

Anger. By definition: a strong feeling of being upset or annoyed; displeasure, or hostility. In Colossians, Paul writes about some of the struggles that we face in this world that we must overcome, anger included. Colossians 3:7-8 says, *"In these you too once walked, when you were living in them. But now you must put them all away: anger, wrath, malice, slander, and obscene talk from your mouth."* When Paul writes "In these you too once walked," he is referring to the past. Therefore, it is not something that we ought to still be living in and practicing. Why? That is where verses 3:9-11 comes in *"Do not lie to one another, seeing that you have put off the old self with its practices and have put on the new self, which is being renewed in knowledge after the image of its Creator. Here there is not Greek and Jew, circumcised and uncircumcised, barbarian, Scythian, slave, free; but Christ is all, and in all."* See, in Christ, we are a new creation. We have put off how we once lived because Christ now lives in us. As followers of Christ, it does not matter who or what you identified, as before, for now, we are His, and He is in us.

I think if we are all honest, we have all struggled in one of these areas that Paul wrote about. For me, anger was something that I struggled with. Although my anger towards my parents that day did not last long, it has always been easier for me to be angry toward them versus other people. As followers of Christ, we cannot forget who we are in Him. Being a Christian is not simply a title, it is our identity, and it is who we are. We cannot take off our "Christian hat" when we feel like it. Just as Paul wrote, Christ is all and in all. We must remember that we have put off our old self and taken on our new identity in Christ. Therefore, we must do our best to reflect and glorify Him in all we do.

Yes, it is easy to become angry with those we love. I know because I have been there and I still struggle with it at times. I want to leave you with this challenge: next time you are angered with someone at work, school, or especially with family, remember the One who is in you and let the anger of your old self go.

2

LUST

Pastor Jayson Combs | Family Pastor

Today it was announced that Angelina Jolie has filed for divorce. Of course, this is not a shock to any of us, but this is one of the most celebrated marriages and families in entertainment. I have a tendency to almost look at Brad Pitt and Angelina Jolie as a fairy tale, but when it comes down to it, there is a man and woman who are broken. There are three children, Shiloh, Vivienne, and Knox, who will be trying to figure out when mom or dad will be around.

What would you say are the top five (5) reasons for divorce in our country? _money, affairs_

Matthew 5:27-30
"You have heard that it was said, 'You shall not commit adultery.' 28 But I say to you that everyone who looks at a woman with lustful intent has already committed adultery with her in his heart. 29 If your right eye causes you to sin, tear it out and throw it away. For it is better that you lose one of your members than that your whole body be thrown

into hell. 30 And if your right hand causes you to sin, cut it off and throw it away. For it is better that you lose one of your members than that your whole body go into hell."

How would you define "lustful intent?" Is it sin to merely gaze upon a man or women? Explain. _____
_____
_____
_____

If lustful looking is so grievous a sin, then those who dress and expose themselves with the desire to be looked at and lusted after... are in sin. (An exposition of the Sermon on the Mount, Baker)

What would you say to someone who says, "I've already committed sin in my mind, so I might as well commit sin with my body?"
_____
_____
_____

1 John 2:16
"For all that is in the world—the desires of the flesh and the desires of the eyes and pride of life—is not from the Father but is from the world."

What are the three areas "lusts of the world" that John describes?
- *desire of the flesh*
- *desire of the eyes*
- *pride of life*

Take time to define each area.

1. To Feel:

_____
_____
_____
_____

2. To Have:

_____
_____
_____
_____

3. To Be:

_____
_____
_____
_____

How many of your top ten reasons for divorce would you say fall into one of those three categories? _____

_____
_____
_____

Where do you see these temptations in your life? Which one do you feel is the biggest? _____

_____
_____
_____
_____

Do you feel these temptations are affecting your family? If so, how? _____
_____
_____

James 1:14-15

"But each person is tempted when he is lured and enticed by his own desire. Then desire when it has conceived gives birth to sin, and sin when it is fully grown brings forth death."

What does James 1:14-15 tell us are the consequences of sin? How do you feel this speaks directly to families? *death —*
The death of the family occurs when you give into sin

Back in Matthew 5, Jesus told people how to deal with lust. Why do you think He made such an over the top statement? _____
_____
_____

Looking at the next few verses, how does God give us instruction to deal with lust? What are some practical ways you can accomplish this? _____
_____
_____

Colossians 3:5

"Put to death therefore what is earthly in you sexual immorality, impurity, passion, evil desire, and covetousness, which is idolatry."

2 Timothy 2:22
"So flee youthful passions and pursue righteousness, faith, love, and peace, along with those who call on the Lord from a pure heart."

Romans 13:14
"But put on the Lord Jesus Christ, and make no provision for the flesh, to gratify its desires."

1 John 2:17
"And the world is passing away along with its desires, but whoever does the will of God abides forever."

Galatians 5:16
"But I say, walk by the Spirit, and you will not gratify the desires of the flesh."

What does it mean to flee from youthful lust? How does that practically apply to your life? _____
_____
_____
_____

How do we walk in the Spirit and not gratify the flesh?
Stay in the Word – Covered in prayer

I want to encourage you to memorize one of these verses. Print it out and put it in your car, on your desk, on your bathroom mirror. If we are going to learn to fight lust, we must learn to *"hide His word in our heart so that we might not sin."*

LUST: DEVOTION 1

EYE "SOUR" CANDY

Debbie Kerr | Office Administrator

"*For all that is in the world-the lust of the flesh, the lust of the eyes and the pride of life-is not of the Father but is of the world.*" I John 2:16 NKJV

The Urban Dictionary defines lust as a "purely physical attraction that has no lasting effect." Have you ever wanted something so badly you just could not get it off your mind and with little regard to the financial ramifications, you finally purchased the item you could not live without, only to find that it really did not deliver the desired feeling you had hoped for? It most likely did for a short time, but it quickly lost its appeal. TV commercials feed into our lusts and now it has crossed over onto the internet and social media. Advertisements are everywhere to catch our eye and make us feel like our life will be complete and fulfilled because our desires will be satisfied. Lust is based on a lie; it is a cheap imitation of the real thing! Lust will not only leave you empty, but it will also rob you of many things. Many marriages are destroyed because of lust; people go bankrupt trying to keep up with the Joneses. People often think they are quickly falling in love when in reality they are falling in lust. Lust is closely related to greed, pride, and it serves itself!

The verses in 1 John 2:16 warn us that the lust of the flesh (I want) the lust of the eyes (I see) the pride of life (I deserve) are not of the Father but of the world. We are very easily seduced by the world system that tells us there is something we are missing that will make us happier. Jesus said in John 10:10, **"The thief comes only to steal, kill and destroy but I have come that they might have life and have it abundantly."** Although the enemy promises us a lot, he cannot "give" us anything. He steals, kills, and destroys. Jesus said He is the giver of the abundant life. When we seek God's desires and lay down our own that is the moment we will feel completely satisfied and fulfilled. Our needs and desires will change as we find our identity in Christ alone. Psalm 37:4 says, **"Delight yourself in the Lord, and He will give you the desires of your heart."** Pray and ask God to help you delight in Him and to change your desires; that is the only place you will find true lasting happiness.

LUST: DEVOTION 2

THE CONVERSATION

Philip Piasecki | Worship Leader

Within the family, lust is something that we do not like to discuss. I remember when I was 12 my dad sat me down to explain to me why we are not supposed to look at certain things. It was not a fun conversation. I am sure he did not enjoy it, but it was an important conversation to have. One day I will have to sit my own children down and explain to them how things that the world says is ok to lust after goes against what the Bible teaches us. Within the family, we have to be willing to sit down and have tough conversations with each other, even when it is uncomfortable.

Lust is something that every person struggles with in some form, and it is something that the Bible speaks about frequently. Romans 8:6 says, *"For to set the mind on the flesh is death, but to set the mind on the Spirit is life and peace."* There are multiple definitions of lust. One form means a "very strong sexual desire," but another definition also means "a passionate desire for something." The Bible warns us in Romans 8:6 about the consequences of having "a passionate desire" for things of the flesh. James 1:14-15 also echoes the same warning, *"But each person is tempted when he is lured and enticed by his own desire. Then desire when it has conceived gives birth to sin, and sin when it is fully grown brings forth death."* When we lust after the things of this world, death is the outcome. The world tells us we should desire power, fame, and money. However, Christ commands us to desire Him and to set our mind on the Spirit. Desiring the things of Christ and not the things of this world is not an easy task. We are constantly bombarded with worldly things everywhere we look.

We need to constantly be aware of the primary things we find ourselves desiring. If we are lusting after things of the flesh, we need to repent and turn our desires towards the things of Christ. The family needs to be there to lift each other up and help one another desire the things of Christ. Parents, you need to show your kids in Scripture the spiritual things they should be desiring. Kids, encourage your siblings to seek after Christ and not the "treasures" of this world. The world trains us to lust after fleshly things; we need to be diligent in strengthening our relationship with Christ each and every day so that our desires will match the desires of His heart. When we make Christ a priority in our lives, we will find ourselves desiring the things He desires. Also, when we make Christ a priority we are setting an example for our family on how they need to live their lives. If we desire life and peace, we must constantly be setting our minds on the things of Christ.

LUST: DEVOTION 3

KEEP YOUR EYES TO YOURSELF

Pastor Ryan Story | Student Pastor

On April 5, 2014, I entered into a covenant with my wife. I promised her that she "would be my lawfully wedded wife, to have and to hold, from this day forward, for better, for worse, for richer, for poorer, in sickness and in health, until death do us part." Most people probably said very similar things. Now we could chat all day long about how broken our society is, and how marriage is no longer what it was "back in the day." The reality is marriages fall apart inside the church at about the same rate that they do outside of it. Now, I am a novice in the husband game. The amount of stupid things I still do makes every "marriage veteran" shake their head. However, there is one thing I have always sworn I would do, and that is to uphold the covenant I made with my wife.

Lust destroys people plain and simple. It destroys young people, old people, married people, single people, men, and women. Teenagers who are never taught proper Godly self-control grow up to become adults who struggle with the exact thing. Whenever I am faced with a problem in my spiritual walk, I always try to go to the root. Think about the last time you had weeds in your yard. It does you no good to spray or just to cut them; you have to yank it out by its root to get rid of them. In my opinion, the root of the sin known as lust first starts with our eyes. The reality is we are all visually stimulated, and men are worse for wear. Job 31:1 says **"I have made a covenant with my eyes; how then could I gaze at a virgin?"** By no means have I arrived, but if I made a covenant with my wife that she was my one and only, then I had better uphold that in every facet of my being. That means I will honor that covenant by the way I provide for her, stick it out with her during the good and hard times, and the things I look at.

While on my wedding day I may not have said those words, shortly after being married I prayed them to God as a sign that I was serious about my marriage. The world we live in claims that there is "no harm in a glance" and we can "look but don't touch." That is the exact opposite of what the Bible says. We live in a society with a lust problem causing a pornographic epidemic, and it is ruining families. Let us be honest; that problem is hurting families inside the church.

"If a woman sees her husband's eyes also affirming the beauty of another woman, she ceases to feel special." I always want to make sure my wife knows how beautiful I think she is, so I never want to leave a time bomb in her mind that will cause her pain. Simply put, if you struggle with "keeping your eyes to yourself," remember this, the moment you married your wife she became the standard of beauty for the rest your life. Stare at some clouds, look at your shoes, or look at the time. Remember, you entered not only a covenant with her, but with God.

LUST: DEVOTION 4

CLEAR THE STAGE

Debbie Gabarra | Community Center Director

All through the Bible, God uses examples of lust and adultery to teach us about how He feels when we put other things before Him.

Lust: a passion or overmastering desire or craving, desire; inclination; wish

Jesus teaches in Matthew 5:28 that if you look with your eyes lustfully, you have sinned in your heart.

2 Samuel 11 sounds so casual as it begins the story of King David's lust and adultery with Bathsheba. ***"It happened, late one afternoon... that he saw from the roof a woman..."*** That look from the roof would begin a journey of incredible sin and sadness. David tried but could not cover his sin. He stole another man's wife, committed murder, and lost a child to death. Remember, God called David a man after His own heart. However, when we seek things that are against the ways of God, it can lead to hurt and destruction that we never imagined.

I recently came across a song, "Clear the Stage" by Jimmy Needham, that begs us to put aside everything that gets in the way of our relationship with God. It challenges us to do whatever it takes to clear from our lives the things that our flesh craves, seek the Lord, and wait for what He has in store us.

The lyrics from "Clear the Stage," suggest some ways to examine our lives.

"Take a break from all the plans that you have made
and sit at home alone and wait for God to whisper.
Beg Him please to open up His mouth and speak,
and pray for real upon your knees until they blister.
Shine the light on every corner of your life
until the pride and lust and lies are in the open.
Then read the Word and put to test the things you've heard,
until your heart and soul are stirred and rocked and broken.
Then seek the Lord and wait for what he has in store,
and know that great is your reward so just be hopeful."

What do you need to clear from your life to make God first?

Jesus said in Matthew 26:41, **"Watch and pray that you may not enter into temptation. The spirit indeed is willing, but the flesh is weak."**

"The LORD is my strength and my shield; in Him my heart trusts, and I am helped." Psalm 28:7a

LUST: DEVOTION 5

DESIRES OF THE HEART
Katrina Young | Nursery & Pre-K Director

*"*__B__*ut each person is tempted when he is lured and enticed by his own desire. Then desire when it has conceived gives birth to sin, and sin when it is fully grown brings forth death."* James 1:14-15

I once heard a pastor teach on lust and the desires of the heart. The emphasis was that "anything that distracts you enough to pull you away from your focus on God is something that you desire more; therefore, you are lusting after that thing." As a new believer, that statement influenced me and still does today. There are so many things in this world set up to distract us, and once distracted we are vulnerable to temptation and ultimately sin.

We live in an age of technology. We do not go anywhere without our phones. From anywhere and at any time we can check e-mail, bank account, social media, or purchase something on Amazon. Ads are everywhere and geared to sell and appeal to our senses. We are constantly being lured to purchase the latest and greatest thing. What effect is this having on our relationship with God? The enemy wants nothing more than for our thoughts to be consumed with enticing things of this world and to distract and pull us away from the things of God. The verse in James tells us **"the desire when it is conceived gives birth to sin."**

Psalms 37:4 says, **"Delight yourself in the Lord and He will give you the desires of your heart."** When we truly "delight" in the things of God, our desires will begin to parallel with His, and we will never go unfulfilled. Matthew 6:33 says, **"But seek first the kingdom of God and his righteousness, and all these things will be added to you."** We will never be deeply fulfilled with the things this world has to offer. It is only when we place our joy and hope in Him that all of our desires will be met.

LUST: DEVOTION 6

DEAR ME

Noble Baird | Guest Services Director

Seven years ago, in my high school psychology class, I wrote a letter to my future self. Our teacher made us do this to parallel a study we were doing in our class. I received my letter back in February of this year and was surprised and delighted at what my younger self was so concerned about for my future. Of course I made mention of old friends and different aspirations I had hoped for in the future, some of which I had succeeded in, others went to the wayside over the years. One note in particular that I was delighted to read about was my concern for my faith. I was concerned that I would not stay the course and endure through whatever was to come.

Whenever one hears the term "lust," it is usually used regarding a sexual nature. If we take a look at the Greek word for lust, "epithumia," it is defined as a desire, passionate longing, and lust. In Titus 3:3-5 Paul writes, ***"For we ourselves were once foolish, disobedient, led astray, slaves to various passions and pleasures, passing our days in malice and envy, hated by others and hating one another. But when the goodness and loving kindness of God our Savior appeared, He saved us."***

Although I was able to write my future self a letter, I wish I could do the same now to myself back when I was in high school. If I am honest with myself and all of you, one of my greatest struggles in high school was lust. I have always struggled with my body image. All throughout middle school, high school, and even into college I desired to have the "perfect" physique. For years I dealt with jealousy because I was so unhappy with my weight. I can remember many times where I was even mad at God trying to figure out why He did not give me the same body type as all my peers. It was this desire and lusting after the world's image of the "perfect male physique" that ruined me. I had truly become a slave to my desire and lusts for the perfect body.

It is easy to become entrapped in the passions and desires of this world. Whether it is through social media, TV, music, etc., the world is constantly painting a picture and a new standard for the "perfect" image. I fell into this trap. I was caught in the chains of the passions and desires the world had shown me. When I realized God's goodness, kindness, and love, I was able to shake those chains of lust. I was able to see myself not through the world's eyes, but through my Father's.

To my younger self and all of you, I just want to say this...

God made you perfect the way you are. He has made each one of us unique and perfect in His image. Do not worry about what the world says or portrays because we are not called to please this world. Yes, I know it is a struggle, and I know it is not easy, but do not let the desire and want to fulfill the world's standards of a "perfect" body control you. Do not let it ruin your life and make you unhappy, jealous, and angry towards others. Instead, look to the One who has shown you love in a way that you have never experienced before. Look to the One who has shown you goodness and kindness. Look to the One who has saved you.

3

PROMISES

Pastor Chuck Lindsey | Reach Pastor

"Do you promise?" I would ask her. However, despite my juvenile attempts to absolutely ensure that we would go get ice cream, my grandmother would never actually say the words, "I promise." She would often say, "I won't promise because you never know what might happen, but we will go." I find myself saying the same to my children today as they press me for a guarantee.

Promises are commonplace in our world. They are made all day, every day. One promises to follow through with a phone call, another to come back and finish a job, and still another to pay back a loan. There was a time when a man was only as good as his word, and a deal could be struck with a handshake. Perhaps the most solemn oaths taken today are made every Saturday in May, in every church across our nation, as a man and a woman vow to love each other through all that life throws at them. Promises and oaths are made every day; it is the keeping of them that proves to be the problem.

As a kid, my friends and I would often say something to the effect of "I swear it on my mother's life!" to confirm that a thing was true. Today, even in a court of law, a witness is asked to place his hand on the Bible and swear to "tell the truth the whole truth and nothing but the truth" so help him God.

Do you make promises? Who have you made them to? _____
_____
_____
_____

Oaths and promises have existed since the fall of man. When man fell, man began to lie. Right there in the first book of the Bible we see Adam and Eve both implying something other than the truth. Then just a chapter later, we see Cain outright lying as a default reaction to the question God asked. It seems that he did not even have to think about it, he just reacted with a lie.

How easy is it for you to lie? Do you find it easier to lie or tell the truth? _____
_____
_____
_____

Since the fall of man, lying has been our default. As a dad, I have never sat down to show my children how to lie. They instinctively know how to. They "default" to it. In fact, I have to teach them NOT to lie. The Bible tells us that as fallen people our instinct to lie comes from our "father" who is a liar. This is not speaking about your earthly father. He may be a very nice and truthful person. It is speaking about our (pre-Jesus) "spiritual father" the devil. Jesus said this about satan in John 8:44 *"...**he does not stand in the truth, because there is NO TRUTH IN HIM. When he lies, he speaks out of his own character, for he is a liar and the father of lies."* As any child does, we emulate our father. Until a person is adopted into a new family by being born again, that person will emulate their fallen "spiritual father." As a result, lying becomes "normal" and expected, and we see that our society lies with abandon in nearly every area imaginable.

Can you give some examples of promises you have seen people make with no intention of keeping? _____
_____
_____
_____

It is always refreshing and often surprising to meet an honest person. Just watch the face of a store clerk when someone says, "you gave me too much money back." The look of shock says it all. It seems that a legitimately truthful person is as rare these days as a four-leaf clover. It is not impossible to find, but it is not common either. The Scriptures are clear that becoming honest people is a massive part of our growth process. As we become more and more like Jesus, who is "the Truth" we become people who want to tell the truth. We become people who want to be reliable. People who are known for keeping their promises. It is only through the life-changing work of Jesus, His Spirit, and His Word in our lives that we become people who not only care to tell the truth but work hard to do so.

Do you have a desire to be trustworthy? If so, how are you practically becoming trustworthy? _____
_____
_____
_____

As we think about our promises, vows, and oaths to our spouses, our children, our families, etc., we have to realize the issue is character. At the end of the day, whether someone can trust what we say comes down to whether we are trustworthy people. Honest people. Truthful people. This is why Jesus said in Matthew 5:33, ***"But let your 'Yes' be 'Yes,' and your 'No,' 'No.' For whatever is more than these is from the evil one"*** (NKJV). According to our Lord, we are to be people of such character that someone does not NEED a guarantee or promise from us to be sure we will do what we have said. Our "Jesus-like" character should be enough to confirm it.

Have you ever known someone who, because of his or her Jesus-like character could be trusted completely? Who? What gave you such confidence? _____
_____
_____
_____

As a husband, a dad, and a pastor, I strive hard in this area of my life. I want to be known as someone who can be counted on. I want my wife to know that I will not leave her or forsake her (as Jesus promises us), that I will be faithful to her as I have promised, and that when I say something, she can be sure that I will do what I have said. I want my children to know that I will love them, provide for them, and lead them in Him as I have said and that I am a man of my word. I want my church family to know that I will pray for them, lead them as He leads, and pursue a life of godliness. Practically speaking, this means that I will need to be realistic about what I am committing to. I cannot vow to do something that I have uncertainty about keeping. It means that there are many things I should say "no" to because I will not be able to keep that obligation. It means that when I say "yes" I need to see that as an issue of character.

What promises have you made to your spouse, children, and family? List them here: _____
_____
_____
_____

Are you someone who is KNOWN for keeping your word? If not, I would encourage you, right now, to confess that to God who is willing to forgive and to ask for His help. He will give you His Spirit's power to become someone your family, friends, and neighbors can depend on.

How will you begin to keep your word from this point forward?
_____
_____
_____

PROMISES: DEVOTION 1

STANDING ON THE PROMISES

Matt Hatton | Children's Director

A promise is simply a declaration made by someone that something will or will not happen. We make promises to one another to give a peace of mind, ensure security in a difficult time, and to pledge our allegiance where it may be questioned. "I promise to do my homework if I can go to the game." "I promise always to be patient and selfless." "I promise to take the trash out." I cannot count how many promises I have made and kept. I also cannot count how many promises I have made and have not kept. Maybe I do not know how to count in general. The point is that we, humanly speaking, tend to make promises, keep promises, and often break promises. Our word is flawed because we are flawed people. We make predictions with our promises and sometimes those predictions are left empty.

As Joshua was getting older, nearing his final days, he gave a charge to all the leaders of Israel to trust in the promises of God. In Joshua 23:14 the Bible says, ***"And now I am about to go the way of all the earth, and you know in your hearts and souls, all of you, that not one word has failed of all the good things that the Lord your God promised concerning you. All have come to pass for you; not one of them has failed."*** Not only are there promises of God's provision and grace, but there are also the promises of His justice. God does not fail us. God will not fail us. What He says in His Word is true; His promises are true.

The promises of God are much different from the promises of man. The promises of God are eternal, not temporal. The promises of God are not predictions. He knows what He is going to do and does it. God promises Eternal Life for those that believe in Him. He promises forgiveness, Himself as the Holy Spirit, to supply our needs, wisdom, guidance, peace, victory over sin and death, protection, and an end to suffering. God's promises are something we can put our hope in. His promises are something we can stand on. He is the firm foundation that we can place everything in our lives upon.

As God's Word teaches us in Matthew 6, we must be careful with our promises. If we make promises on our own grounds, then they will be flawed and broken. If we live our lives according to God's Word, then our words should be reflective of that. As followers of Christ, we need to be trustworthy people with a trustworthy word because out of our lips we can share the promises of God that are not flawed, broken, or fallible.

My prayer is this: "Lord, thank you for your wonderful promises. Thank you for being a firm foundation that I can build my life upon. Let my words reflect your words. Help me to be an honest and trustworthy person because of my trust in you and your promises."

PROMISES: DEVOTION 2

WORD

Philip Piasecki | Worship Leader

My brother is currently a missionary in the country of Oman in the Middle East. Last year before he left the country, he decided that he wanted to get a tattoo of Michigan. I had always wanted a tattoo as well, so I thought getting one together before he leaves would be an awesome brotherly bonding experience. We came up with a plan and agreed to get them together. The only problem was that when he called me to tell me he was at the tattoo shop I bailed. I came up with every excuse in the book on why I could not get a tattoo. Luckily, he had another friend with him who got the tattoo alongside him. I am sure he is still a little upset with me that I bailed, and I do not blame him. Now, if I ever agree to do something like that with him again, he is never going to believe me.

Scripture says in James 5:12, ***"But above all, my brothers, do not swear, either by heaven or by earth or by any other oath, but let your "yes" be yes and your "no" be no, so that you may not fall under condemnation."*** When we make a promise, we need to keep that promise. For some reason, Christians are viewed as some of the flakiest people, and I think it is for good reasons. Our actions and behaviors reflect Christ, and one of the simplest ways to positively reflect Christ is to be a reliable person. If a friend asks you to help them move and you say yes, then show up on the day of the move. If you tell your kid that you are going to take them to the park tomorrow, follow through and actually take them. Kids, if you tell your parents you are going to get your chores done, do them. When we honor our word, we are honoring Christ. It is a powerful testimony when someone knows that if you tell him or her you are going to do something that you will follow through with it. An area where this issue is painfully evident is within serving in the church.

The body of Christ relies on believers serving, and we put the Church leadership in impossible situations when we agree to serve and then do not follow through on it. Serve Christ, and be committed to it. If you agree to serve in the nursery, do not cancel Sunday morning. In whatever area you have agreed to serve, there is an eternal difference waiting to be made; you just need to follow through on your word. We need to reflect the character of Christ by being people who follow through on our promises. We have a God who never breaks His promises. We know that we can count on Him no matter what the circumstance is, and as followers of Christ, we should be able to be counted on in the same manner.

PROMISES: DEVOTION 3

ONLY YES OR NO

Pastor Ryan Story | Student Pastor

When I first started at The River Church, my role was "Student Disicpler." Now discipler is not even a word, but nonetheless, that is what Pastor Jim called me. One of my major responsibilities was to seek out high school and middle school boys who were looking to take their walk with Jesus further. I had one middle school boy who taught me a valuable lesson. After the first year was concluding, I told a few of the middle school boys that I would take them to Cooks Farm Dairy for some ice cream. I had the best intentions in mind. I knew where all of them lived, all of their parents were on board, and I just needed to pick a day. Sadly, the busyness of life never allowed me to fulfill my promise. Now one would think that a 12-year-old's memory would be foggy, but not this dude. Every so often, I would hear "you haven't taken us out to ice cream."

As people, we always have a tendency to overcommit to things. I know I do that with people in the church, my wife, and I will probably do that with my own kids someday. I feel that people, at times, have very good intentions. When I said I would take those boys out, I meant it and wanted to do so. Jesus says, **"Let what you say be simply 'Yes' or 'No'; anything more than this comes from evil"** (Matthew 5:37). I feel that we all need to look at our commitment level in our lives. Sadly, I know when I start to overcommit, I commit to the things that do not matter as much. When I overcommit I commit to things that are not always bad, but they are not what is best. Jesus says it perfectly (as He always does); do not say "yes" unless you can fulfill that promise. Some of us work demanding jobs, go to school, and live lives where there is a ton to do. Take some time next time you make a promise to realize there are only two options to that choice. Yes or no. I feel we all live in the I said yes, but I will get around to it. I tell my wife I am going to do the laundry, eventually. That is not exactly living up to that promise. I am sure you can think of a few of those scenarios in your life.

That boy is now going into 10th grade. Every summer the two of us set a few weeks aside to do a Bible study. I was tired of feeling like a man who was all talk and just promised things. I am glad he always brought up that I was not true to my word. This year on our last meeting I took him to lunch and then to Cooks Farm Dairy. As I was dropping him off at his house, he looked at me, said "about time", and then said "thanks." I do not know why I felt God kind of give me a pat on the back and say, "He will never forget this story." Take some time today to think about some of the promises that you have made. Take a lesson from God that if He always delivers on His promise that means you have to as well. Remember we will be remembered; hopefully, we are all remembered as someone who keeps our promises.

PROMISES: DEVOTION 4

HE KEEPS HIS PROMISES

Kyle Wendel | Children & Student's Director

Have you ever made a promise to someone before? I am sure we can all think at least some goofy promise we made before. I know my mom used to tell me as a kid that if I ate my green beans, I would become the green power ranger. Unfortunately, I have not transformed into him just yet… hopefully, someday that will come true!

Promises that we humans make fall short a lot. We often make promises we cannot keep. We end up breaking those promises and often hurting someone. However, the promises of the Lord will never be broken or come up void. They will always be true and come in full.

Let us just look at a few promises that God has given us that have not been broken.

Deuteronomy 31:8 says, ***"It is the Lord who goes before you. He will be with you; he will not leave you or forsake you. Do not fear or be dismayed."***

How awesome is it to think about how the Lord is always with us and will never leave or forsake us?! You may not always be able to rely on other people's promises, but you can always know the Lord will never leave your side. He is always there for you. He will never break His promise.

Romans 8:28 says, ***"And we know that for those who love God all things work together for good, for those who are called according to his purpose."***

All things work together for those who love God. Now this does not mean everything in our earthly lives will go the best in our thoughts. We often are too caught up in the here and now. However, in the eyes of God, the things will work out for good for us. We can have closer fellowship with God, bearing fruit for the kingdom, and we will one day be with God.

2 Corinthians 1:20 says, ***"For all the promises of God find their Yes in him. That is why it is through him that we utter our Amen to God for his glory."***

All God's promises find their fulfillment in Christ. The Old Testament promises and prophecies point to Jesus. Christ fulfills them all. He has given God's Word weight to them. How amazing is it to think about all the things Christ has fulfilled for us. It is crazy that we know that God's promises are so true and will never come up short. We know that we can always trust His word. We can always trust His promises to us. Let us never doubt God and His word. Let us hold fast to Him.

PROMISES: DEVOTION 5

WE'LL GO TOMORROW, I PROMISE

John Hubbard | Worship Leader

"Come now, you who say, 'Today or tomorrow we will go into such and such a town and spend a year there and trade and make a profit'— yet you do not know what tomorrow will bring. What is your life? For you are a mist that appears for a little time and then vanishes. Instead you ought to say, 'If the Lord wills, we will live and do this or that.' As it is, you boast in your arrogance. All such boasting is evil." James 4:13-16

I wish that I could keep my promises, especially to my family, but the truth is that more often than not I cannot control when things are going to happen. My daughter is nearly three years old, and even at this age, it is a crushing defeat when I cannot take her on a fun playdate because something else has come up that I cannot ignore. James writes that to plan our lives without acknowledging the Lord's will is to boast in our arrogance. This sounds easy enough, to remember God's sovereignty, but how often do we plan and schedule our time or save and spend our money without thinking about what the Lord's will is in our life?

Our lives are like a mist. It is a glimpse in the span of eternity. If you ever tried telling your mom what she will be making you for dinner when you were younger, you have a pretty good idea about how foolish it is to make plans without acknowledging the Creator of all things as at the very least a factor in your decision-making process. Now sometimes your mom might let you pick what is for dinner, and sometimes God will let you pick what you might do as well. Just keep in mind that sometimes, it is just not up to you.

PROMISES: DEVOTION 6

HIGHER STANDARDS

Noble Baird | Guest Services Director

Three years ago, I made a promise to my future wife and family. You see, I do not take titles lightly. Whether that title is pastor, officer, doctor, sergeant, etc. they are all titles that are to be respected. Uncle Ben from Spider-Man said, "With great power comes great responsibility." Just as I have much respect for those who hold certain titles, I also hold them to a higher standard. With that being said, I believe that the titles of husband and father are the two most privileged titles a man can ever receive. That is why I made a promise to my future wife and family. I promised them that I was going to get my act together, get healthy, set my priorities straight, not conform, and continually seek after God to become the man they will need.

Paul also knew the gravity of these titles. In Ephesians 5:25 he writes, **"Husbands, love your wives, as Christ loved the church and gave himself up for her."** I do not know about the rest of you, but when Paul uses Christ as the example for a life lesson, I think it is important. You see, Paul says that Christ's relationship with us, the Church, is the same relationship that husbands and wives ought to be modeled after. Paul is setting the benchmark high with this passage. He is not taking the title of husband lightly, so why do we?

All too often in social media, TV, the news, books, etc. the world is changing and reshaping the standard. For example, nowadays it is often acceptable and encouraged for couples to have premarital sex. Reason being, relationships are like used cars, and you have to "test-drive" it before you buy. Another one that I see often is the whole I would rather them drink alcohol in my house rather than out at a friend's or some party; since breaking one law and starting a bad habit will not lead to another, right? You see, our society has corrupted and changed Christ's standard and His example to what the world deems acceptable and true.

That is why I made the promise. Know my heart; I am not saying that I am best or a model of Christ in every aspect of my life because truthfully I am not. I mess up daily. However, I do my best to continually chase after the example, the model, and the standard that Paul writes about and Christ set. Christ loves us, the Church, so much that He laid down His life for us. He sacrificed and made Himself a servant out of love. That is why I promised to do the same. I know that I am going to mess up and fail, I am human, and I am not perfect. Yet, when Paul writes to husbands and all the future husbands, he is leaving them with more than just a challenge; he is giving them the standard.

So, instead of a challenge, I want to leave you men with this question: have you been chasing after Christ's standard in your marriage and family? Or have you conformed to the standard that the world has deemed acceptable?

4

RETALIATION
John Sanchez

In Matthew Chapter 5, Jesus delivers His famous Sermon on the Mount. In this chapter, Jesus poetically inspires and challenges His disciples. It is within this chapter that we find the familiar 'turn the other cheek' passage. A passage that, if we are totally honest, is hard to swallow. It offends our natural human tendency to retaliate against injuries and offenses committed against us or those closest to us.

"You have heard that it was said, 'An eye for an eye and a tooth for a tooth.'" Matthew 5:38

The term 'eye for an eye' is pretty widely recognized. Though most people would think this term originated from the Bible, it actually predates Jesus by over 1700 years. Originally part of the Babylonian Empire's code of law, its intent was to administer justice in matters of government. To ensure that the penalty issued for a crime did not exceed the degree of the offense. As we would say today, "let the punishment fit the crime."

In this passage, Jesus was most likely directly referring to the Law as written in Deuteronomy: ***"If a malicious witness arises to accuse a person of wrongdoing, then both parties to the***

dispute shall appear before the LORD, before the priests and the judges who are in office in those days. The judges shall inquire diligently, and if the witness is a false witness and has accused his brother falsely, then you shall do to him as he had meant to do to his brother. So you shall purge the evil from your midst. And the rest shall hear and fear, and shall never again commit any such evil among you. Your eye shall not pity. It shall be life for life, eye for eye, tooth for tooth, hand for hand, foot for foot." Deuteronomy 19:16-21

Does this passage in the Old Testament seem to contradict Jesus' teaching in Matthew 5? _____
_____
_____
_____

To whom is the decree of 'eye for an eye' being given to in this passage (Verses 17-18)? _____
_____
_____
_____

Have you ever experienced mistreatment, injustice, or offenses from others? _____
_____
_____
_____

If you are a parent, have you experienced the same toward your children or family? _____
_____
_____

What is our natural inclination when we find ourselves in these situations? _____

_____

_____

_____

A quick read through Deuteronomy 19 reveals this decree was directed and intended for those responsible for administering justice in the land. In Matthew 5, Jesus is speaking directly to the people of Israel when referencing the 'eye for an eye' decree. Matthew Henry's commentary on this passage indicates the Jewish teachers of the time had usurped the divine intent of this principal and propagated the idea that those who were wronged were fully justified in taking the law into their own hands. It is not difficult to see how this errant teaching fed into the human heart's inclination to seek its own revenge in matters of offense.

In situations where we find ourselves justifiably wronged and offended, what should be our response? Who should we ultimately leave the matter of justice to? _____

_____

_____

"That old law about 'an eye for an eye' leaves everybody blind. The time is always right to do the right thing." - Martin Luther King, Jr.

Jesus goes on to challenge the status quo:

"But I say to you, Do not resist the one who is evil. But if anyone slaps you on the right cheek, turn to him the other also. And if anyone would sue you and take your tunic, let

him have your cloak as well. And if anyone forces you to go one mile, go with him two miles. Give to the one who begs from you, and do not refuse the one who would borrow from you." Matthew 5:39-42

What are some immediate thoughts or reactions you have after reading these verses? Do you think the disciples also felt the same reactions? Why? _____
_____
_____
_____

As a young Christian, I can recall first reading this passage. I remember feeling confused, wondering why God would require us to allow others to hurt us, abuse us, and take advantage of us. Maybe you are wondering the same thing. Jesus' message is made clear when we step back and consider the entirety of the chapter. To understand the message, me must first know and understand the messenger. To understand the messenger, we must immerse ourselves into the message.

What was Jesus' primary mission coming to earth? What do these verses reveal about Jesus and our Heavenly Father? (John 3:16, Romans 5:8, 1 John 4:9-11) _____
_____
_____
_____

To understand the message, we must first understand the heartbeat of the messenger. Let's dive into God's Word (the message) to understand God's Word.

Verse 39a: ***"But I say to you, Do not resist the one who is evil. But if anyone slaps you on the right cheek, turn to him the other also."***

How can we understand this verse by reading Matthew 5:9? _____
_____
_____

Does God value retaliation or reconciliation? _____
_____
_____
_____

Verses 40: ***"And if anyone would sue you and take your tunic, let him have your cloak as well."***

Luke's account is a bit different. Read Luke 6:29. What is the difference? _____
_____
_____

In biblical times, a tunic was an inexpensive undergarment. A person's cloak was a larger outer garment which was worn for warmth, protection, and also used as a
blanket at night – a much more valuable possession. Under Mosaic law, it was unlawful to take a person's outer garment overnight (Read Exodus 22:26-27; Deuteronomy 24:12-13).

How can we understand verse 40 properly by reading the following verses (1 Corinthians 9:15,19)? _____
_____
_____

Did Paul concern himself with what was 'fair', or did he consider something else supremely more important? Did Paul retaliate by aggressively asserting his rights or by patiently leaving room for understanding to grow? _____

_____

_____

Can exercising love and patience put us in jeopardy of being taken advantage of? _____

_____

_____

Verse 41: **"And if anyone forces you to go one mile, go with him two miles."**

We have all heard the familiar saying, "Go the extra mile." Consider the truth we try to communicate with that saying. This term most likely struck a raw nerve for the Jews during Jesus' time. Roman soldiers were allowed to demand a subject to carry their equipment for one mile. This was no small load; as some scholars have suggested, this could have easily been 100 pounds. Earlier in this chapter (Matthew 5:20), Jesus tells the disciples that their righteousness must 'exceed that of the scribes and Pharisees' to enter into the Kingdom of Heaven. What was He trying to say there? _____

_____

_____

Jesus also says, in verse 17, **"Do not think that I have come to abolish the Law or the Prophets; I have not come to abolish them but to fulfill them."**

How could the disciples ensure their righteousness exceeded that of the scribes and Pharisees as Jesus admonished? How could we do that today? _____

_____

If the Pharisees primary motivation was to govern and restrict outward behavior to comply with the Law, what was Jesus' primary motivation that enabled him to fulfill the law?

_____

_____

How does our developing love for God and people affect our attitude and behavior towards those who hurt, offend, or selfishly assert themselves against us? Does God's love show itself in the least amount of effort and care, or does it labor to communicate itself in the grandest way? _____

_____

_____

Verse 42: ***"Give to the one who begs from you, and do not refuse the one who would borrow from you."***

Giving and lending can be sour subjects for us. Have you ever had a friend or neighbor borrow something and forget to give it back? Have you ever done the same? _____

_____

_____

Most of us avoid asking for it to be returned, not wanting to come across as stingy, so we allow anger and bitterness to fester in us over the whole ordeal. However, God's love prompts us to respond differently toward our neighbor with a genuine need. Our acts of service and giving (or lack thereof) do not go unnoticed by our Heavenly Father. Read the following verses.

Deuteronomy 15:7-10
Proverbs 21:26
Proverbs 28:27
Luke 3:11
Acts 20:35

We have all heard the phrase, "actions speak louder than words." Can you think of any other way God's love can shout louder than giving? _____
_____
_____
_____

We should be giving our time, talent, treasure, and ourselves. John 3:16a tells us 'For God so loved the world that he gave....' Jesus consistently admonishes us to rise above ourselves, and our natural inclinations, to a higher place. It is only through Him that we can allow God's love to work in and through us. Retaliation only leads to escalation, but God's love gives room for reconciliation. Isn't that what Jesus is all about?

If we belong to Him, should we make room for reconciliation as well? _____
_____
_____
_____

Who should you reconcile with now? _____
_____
_____
_____

Pray for them.

How will you contact them (letter, email, text, face-to-face)?

When will you contact them?

RETALIATION: DEVOTION 1

DON'T RETALIATE, BLESS

Isaiah Combs | Worship Leader & Young Adults Director

I would say I am a hot-tempered person. During my early teens to my early 20s, I developed a no-nonsense reputation. My reputation was built on my temper and repaying people's negative action toward me. Whether that was with words or actions, I was not to be shown up. I made it very clear to people that I was not afraid to retaliate, and I would let my temper get the best of me. It did not take much to set me off. I am sorry to say that I hurt many people, and I was not the light I was supposed to be.

I know I am not the only one that struggles with anger and retaliations. Anger is not the sin. Ephesians 4:26 says, **"Be angry and do not sin."** Even Jesus was angry in Matthew 21:12, **"And Jesus entered the temple and drove out all who sold and bought in the temple, and he overturned the tables of the money-changers and the seats of those who sold pigeons."** Jesus was angry, but He did not sin.

Retaliation is the sin. My retaliation to a word being said to me or actions being done to me has been less than Jesus-like. I have been kicked out of countless games due to retaliation against other players and referees. I believe it was only Jesus who saved me from getting into serious trouble in the military from letting my temper get the best of me. I also need to thank you, Lord, for my wife who has dealt with my anger and me for a long time.

I have learned that Jesus is the only way to help me with my anger. The Bible has many verses about the right response to anger. Proverbs 15:1-4 says, **"A soft answer turns away wrath, but a harsh word stirs up anger."** James 1:19 says, **"Know**

this, my beloved brothers: let every person be quick to hear, slow to speak, slow to anger."

Peter was a man known to lose his temper. He was quick to open his mouth and quick to draw his sword. However, Peter was changed and forgiven by Jesus. 1 Peter 3:9 says, ***"Do not repay evil for evil or reviling for reviling, but on the contrary, bless, for to this you were called, that you may obtain a blessing."***

It is hard to repay blessing for evil. It is much easier to blow up. Yes, they probably deserve it. Yes, wives and kids can press the buttons that tend to put you in a place you never thought you could be. Yes, I know people love to run their mouths. Yes, it takes work. Yes, you feel weird. But...Bless them that you may obtain a blessing. The blessings of God are much more satisfying than the satisfaction of retaliation.

Do Not Retaliate, Bless.

RETALIATION: DEVOTION 2

I FOR AN EYE

Philip Piasecki | Worship Leader

Have you ever been driving down the road and a car passes you going significantly above the speed limit? I am sure that has happened before, and you have probably had similar thoughts to mine. "Man, I hope that guy gets pulled over." Then a couple of minutes later, boom! You drive by that person as they are handing their license and registration over to that state trooper. You know that person is getting their due punishment. Anyone going 100 MPH on the freeway deserves a ticket. However, that punishment is not something that is for us to decide. It takes a police officer to hand out that punishment.

In the same way, vengeance and retaliation towards sin is something that is not in our control, but it is God's responsibility. Romans 12:17-21 says, **"Repay no one evil for evil, but give thought to do what is honorable in the sight of all. If possible, so far as it depends on you, live peaceably with all. Beloved, never avenge yourselves, but leave it to the wrath of God, for it is written, 'Vengeance is mine, I will repay, says the Lord.' To the contrary, 'if your enemy is hungry, feed him; if he is thirsty, give him something to drink; for by so doing you will heap burning coals on his head.' Do not be overcome by evil, but overcome evil with good."**

Scripture instructs us that vengeance is not ours to be had. We are not to retaliate with evil when we are sinned against. This is a command that feels so unnatural because our sin nature desires that we get revenge ourselves when we are wronged. Scripture tells us that we should actually meet the needs of our enemies instead of getting revenge. When we take this instruction and apply it to our own families, it hits even closer to home. If my wife does something that upsets me, I have no right to turn around and "pay her back" for what she has done. I am instructed to love her and forgive her. When we think about our relationships, we need to look at the example Christ gives us with the Church. Believers continually sin against God, yet He continues to love and forgive us. We need to apply that same love and forgiveness to those who wrong us in our lives. If a family member has hurt you, you need to love them. If a family member has sinned against you, you need to forgive them. There are people in this world who have done terrible things, and we can trust that God will deal with them in the way that He sees fit. Vengeance is not our job, and I am glad for that. We get the privilege of reflecting Christ's love to a broken and hurting world. Let us strive to do that better and better each and every day.

RETALIATION: DEVOTION 3

SILENT RETALIATION

Pastor Ryan Story | Student Pastor

Think about a time when someone in your family wronged you. Let us be honest, conflict in the family is there. How did you handle that situation? Now as a Christ follower and person who is striving to act like Jesus in every situation that arises, I am sure you handled it in the most God honoring way; eventually. Sadly, whenever a conflict arises in my life, resolution is not the first word that comes to mind. The first word that comes to mind is retaliation. If someone wrongs me, I love running to Deuteronomy 19:21 and declaring that God wants me to exact revenge on those who hurt me. I love using Samson as an example in Judges 15 and burning people's lives down. Now clearly these acts of aggressive retaliation are wrong, sinful, and not Christ-like. If you are one who is overly aggressive to retaliate, that is a dangerous place to be. However, there is a new modern form of retaliation that I feel destroys families at the same extent, just at a slower pace.

Think of a time where you were passively retaliating towards someone. Be honest there was a time you were upset with someone and instead of going to them like Jesus says to (Matthew 18:15-19) you are critical of the person, your humor is hostile at its core, you ignore the person, you become two faced with them, or you just unreasonably blame that person for EVERYTHING. Passive aggressiveness is becoming one of the major pitfalls in God's people's lives. I was searching and searching in the Bible for a good story that could be used as an example of passive retaliation, and it finally dawned on me to look back at the Serpent in the Garden of Eden. Read Genesis 3 sometime and be honest, how often do you act like the Serpent. He tells half-truths. He has an issue with Adam and Eve but never comes out and addresses it.

He is an enemy disguised as a friend. He is "trying to help" but his intentions are hostile to the core. Be honest this is how we handle conflict sometimes, and let us be really honest with ourselves, this is how we handle conflict with our own family.

We live in a world that tries to tell people that conflict is a bad thing, and it should be avoided at all costs. Now I am not advocating all-out war, but why would Jesus discuss conflict management? Clearly, He knew that there would be issues with God's children; clearly, He knew we had to have a better way to deal with issues than just killing each other or cutting them out of our lives. In your family (or your life), who do you need to go chat with? Are your conflict battle tactics ruining your family because you are embodying the enemy instead of our Savior? Take some time this week to undo the mess. Take some time to gain back a family member.

RETALIATION: DEVOTION 4

HOW DO WE RESPOND

Wes McCullough | Worship Leader

Retaliation is an instinctive human response. When someone offends us, our initial reaction is to respond in kind. Sometimes we escalate our response to protect ourselves from another attack to win. However, does God want us to win?

As a young boy, I had an anger control problem. When my sisters upset me, I would lash out physically. Today I thank God for good parents who disciplined me. The result of my discipline was a mentality of considering the consequence of my choice of words and actions. Every choice comes with a consequence. Whether that consequence is good or bad depends on the choice. Everything I say and do is in pursuit of a positive consequence.

The Bible is full of instruction on what kind of choices we should make. When it comes to our words, James 3:6 says the tongue *"corrupts the whole body, sets the whole course of one's body on fire"* (NIV). 1 Peter 3:9 says, *"Don't repay evil for evil. Don't retaliate with insults when people insult you"* (NLT). Proverbs 25:21-22 says, *"If your enemy is hungry, give him bread to eat, and if he is thirsty, give him water to drink."* Matthew 5:40 says, *"And if anyone would sue you and take your tunic, let him have your cloak as well."*

These responses seem impossible to us. Surely our emotions would get the better of us. Why would we have these unbelievable responses to those who have wronged us? Jesus loved us when we did not deserve it. When we had cursed Him, forgotten Him, or disobeyed Him, He responded with unfailing love.

God has called us not to retaliate, but to love. **"Above all, keep loving one another"** (1 Peter 4:8). **"...live peaceably with all"** (Romans 12:18) **"live generously and graciously toward others..."** (Matt. 5:48 MSG). The God of grace and mercy commands us to Love those who oppose us.

Does God want us to win? Yes, but He does not want us to do the fighting. Exodus 14:14 says it plainly, **"The Lord himself will fight for you. Just stay calm"** (NLT). The response God commands us to have may not always seem right, but I certainly believe the all-knowing, all-powerful God can fight my battles better than I can. **"Vengeance is mine...says the Lord"** (Romans 12:19).

RETALIATION: DEVOTION 5

THE POTENTIAL PRISONER

Josh Lahring | Production Director

Over the years, we have had the opportunity to go in Ohio prisons to minister to inmates. While talking with the inmates, some of them will share their story. You will find that many of them are in there because they got revenge on somebody that hurt a friend or a family member. They gave the justice they thought they deserved, and at the end of it all, it destroyed their own life.

At one point or another in our lives, we have been angry enough with someone who hurt us to want to get even. Retaliation ends up hurting us more than what was done to us to begin with. It consumes our thoughts and our life with anger and hate. For some it builds up enough to where they take action, and they will choose to take matters into their own hands.

We have been given an example of how we should treat those who hurt us. If there is anyone who should have retaliated, it is Jesus. He was beat, whipped, spit on, mocked, cursed, and nailed to a cross. Through all of that, He asked God to forgive them. He could have destroyed all of us if He wanted to, but He chose to lay His life down for our sake.

Our attitude should be that of Christ, we should pray for the ones who hurt us. Do not pray that God gives the person what they deserve; pray that He does a work in their lives, and that you can live at peace with them. Remember that God is a Just God, and His ways are beyond our understanding.

Romans 12:17-19 says, **"Repay no one evil for evil, but give thought to do what is honorable in the sight of all. If** *possible, so far as it depends on you, live peaceably with all. Beloved, never avenge yourselves, but leave it to the wrath of God, for it is written, 'Vengeance is mine, I will repay, says the Lord.'"*

RETALIATION: DEVOTION 6

THE WILL OR THY WILL

Noble Baird | Guest Services Director

On February 27, 2013, my grandpa passed away. Sadly, I was away at college when this happened, and I did not get the chance to say goodbye to him. We had a private funeral with just family. However, this was only the beginning of the heartbreak that was to affect my family. My grandpa never left a will behind to specify what would be done with all of his belongings. Having six children, five of which are in state and one that is out, you can imagine how this could be problematic; and it was. Not long after my grandpa's funeral, my mother received a letter from an attorney hired by two of my aunts and my uncle. My mother was the head of my grandpa's estate, which he had put in place years before his passing. This letter was the beginning of what has now been over three-year legal battle.

In Matthew 5:38-42, Jesus talks about this concept of retaliation. He paints a picture of what it physically looks like. In verse 39, He says, *"But I say to you, Do not resist the one who is evil. But if anyone slaps you on the right cheek, turn to him the other also."*

As followers of Christ, we are called to be His example to those around us. Not simply in the way we talk but in every aspect of our lives. Paul tells us this in 1 Timothy 4:12, *"Let no one despise you for your youth, but set the believers an example in speech, in conduct, in love, in faith, in purity."* When Paul was writing this, he was writing to his younger apprentice Timothy. Although it talks about "your youth," this is applicable to all of us as followers of Christ in how we ought to live our lives. We ought to set an example to both believer and non-believers alike, by living a life that is reflective and glorifying Christ.

For me, my mother has been the greatest example of what Jesus teaches here. Throughout the chaos and heartache of this journey my mother has been on, she has endured. Paul writes about this endurance in Romans 5:3-5, **"Not only that, but we rejoice in our suffering, knowing that suffering produces endurance, and endurance produces character, and character produces hope, and hope does not put us to shame, because God's love has been poured into our hearts through the Holy Spirit who has been given to us."** My mother has endured, so that she can be an example of Christ's love to her brother and sisters.

So, how will you react? When someone hurts you, will you retaliate or turn the other cheek? Instead of harsh words, will you pray for them? Instead of raising a fist, will you embrace them in a hug? Remember to endure in the example you are setting in Christ.

DIVORCE

APPENDIX 1

DIVORCE?

DIVORCE

DIVORCE:
WHAT DOES THE BIBLE SAY?
Dr. Randy T. Johnson | Growth Pastor

Ben Carson is a famous neurosurgeon, author, speaker, and politician. He was even the subject for a television drama film. One of the feats that thrust him into the spotlight was when he performed the first and only successful separation of Siamese twins joined at the back of the head. It was an amazing surgery in separating two that had been one. The decision was not taken lightly.

Divorce is very similar. It is the separation of two that had been one. It can not be taken lightly. From the very start of mankind, God created us with the intent of a couple being one. Genesis 2:20-25 says, *"The man gave names to all livestock and to the birds of the heavens and to every beast of the field. But for Adam there was not found a helper fit for him. 21 So the LORD God caused a deep sleep to fall upon the man, and while he slept took one of his ribs and closed up its place with flesh. 22 And the rib that the LORD God had taken from the man he made into a woman and brought her to the man. 23 Then the man said, 'This at last is bone of my bones and flesh of my flesh; she shall be called Woman, because she was taken out of Man.' 24 Therefore a man shall leave his father and his mother and hold fast to his wife, and they shall become one flesh. 25 And the man and his wife were both naked and were not ashamed."* All the animals were created. Adam was given the opportunity to name them all. I think that would have been fun. However, he still felt alone. A dog may be "man's best friend," but God had a better plan. He created woman. As soon as she is created, God makes a declaration, *"A man shall leave his father and his mother and hold fast to his wife, and they shall become one flesh."* God immediately set the groundwork. Children had not been born yet. There were no families yet. However, God had a plan. It included marriage, family, and "becoming one flesh." When children got older they were to find a mate, leave home, and become one with their spouse. There was not any discussion or thought of the "one" splitting up.

It is important to examine God's Word when faced with life's challenges. We need to study these verses to get a proper view of what divorce is. It should be noted: God created marriage; man created divorce. There are five main passages of Scripture that should be examined.

Matthew 19
Matthew 19:3-9 is one of the passages most examined when studying the topic of divorce. It says, *"And Pharisees came up to him and tested him by asking, 'Is it lawful to divorce one's wife for any cause?' 4 He answered, 'Have you not read that he who created them from the beginning made them male and female, 5 and said, 'Therefore a man shall leave his father and his mother and hold fast to his wife, and the two shall become one flesh'? 6 So they are no longer two but one flesh. What therefore God has joined together, let not man separate.' 7 They said to him, 'Why then did Moses command one to give a certificate of divorce and to send her away?' 8 He said to them, 'Because of your hardness of*

heart Moses allowed you to divorce your wives, but from the beginning it was not so. 9 And I say to you: whoever divorces his wife, except for sexual immorality, and marries another, commits adultery.'"

There are four key points here. First, it is the Pharisees who ask the question about divorce, but it is not with a sincere heart. They are not interested in the truth as much as they are about "testing" Jesus. They want to find fault in Him, so they can stay living the way they were. Often people asking about divorce do not really want the truth. Second, Jesus takes them back to creation. He starts with the start. From the beginning they were to **"hold fast"** and be **"one flesh."** He mentions that **"God has joined together."** God created marriage; man created divorce. Third, the Pharisees bring up Moses. People like to know if they are the exemption to the rule. Even in discussing what Moses allowed, Jesus again takes them back to the beginning. Fourth, Jesus brings up an exception clause. Divorce is wrong, but allowed in the case of **"sexual immorality."** It is a devastating blow when an outsider divides the two who have already become one. When one partner becomes one with an someone else, then there are grounds for divorce. Jesus never commanded divorce, but in this case He said it is allowed.

Marriage is a gift from God. It needs to be protected. When one party of the union has an affair, divorce is permitted. However, Scripture consistently teaches forgiveness and reconciliation. An affair should not be used as an excuse to get a divorce. The goal is to flee fornication, not flee because of fornication. Again, forgiveness and reconciliation are the goal.

Matthew 5

Matthew 5:31-32 is another passage used on the topic of divorce, ***"It was also said, 'Whoever divorces his wife, let him give her a certificate of divorce.' But I say to you that everyone who divorces his wife, except on the ground of sexual immorality, makes her commit adultery, and whoever marries a divorced woman commits adultery."*** This passage doesn't really add anything new to the topic. Divorce should not happen, but is permitted in the case of sexual immorality.

1 Corinthians 7

1 Corinthians 7 brings up a new aspect of divorce. Verses 15-17 say, ***"But if the unbelieving partner separates, let it be so. In such cases the brother or sister is not enslaved. God has called you to peace. For how do you know, wife, whether you will save your husband? Or how do you know, husband, whether you will save your wife? Only let each person lead the life that the Lord has assigned to him, and to which God has called him. This is my rule in all the churches."*** A new situation arose in the early church. Men and women were leaving their partner because they were so offended that their partner had gotten saved. They were not committing adultery; they were just leaving. They were separating from them. It was kind of a tough love. They were probably hoping that their newly saved partner would "come to their senses", leave Christianity, and be reunited with them. Early Christians often lost family, friends, and employment due to a "simple" decision to claim Jesus as Messiah and Lord. This really isn't a passage for divorce. It is more about comforting someone who has been left because of his or her faith. God wants them to feel His peace. If an unbeliever leaves, but doesn't remarry, then the believer needs to be faithful in prayer and love hoping their spouse gives their life to the Lord. If an unbeliever leaves and marries or "hooks up" with someone

else, then Matthew 19 is applicable and the person can get a divorce. However, the main goal should be the salvation of the unbelieving partner.

People have twisted this passage to say that if someone gets saved and their partner is not saved, then they can divorce them. The context really emphasizes the importance of marriage. Verses 10-11 say, *"To the married I give this charge (not I, but the Lord): the wife should not separate from her husband (but if she does, she should remain unmarried or else be reconciled to her husband), and the husband should not divorce his wife."* The command is clear that divorce is not an option. Separation may be necessary, but not divorce. Note the word *"reconciled"* is used.

Verses 12-14 are very basic, *"To the rest I say (I, not the Lord) that if any brother has a wife who is an unbeliever, and she consents to live with him, he should not divorce her. If any woman has a husband who is an unbeliever, and he consents to live with her, she should not divorce him. For the unbelieving husband is made holy because of his wife, and the unbelieving wife is made holy because of her husband. Otherwise your children would be unclean, but as it is, they are holy."* If someone gets saved, they do not have the right to divorce the unsaved partner. It is interesting that the passage talks about doing the right thing for the sake of the children. It may not be easy. It may take a long time. But the goal is for their salvation.

Malachi 2
Malachi 2:16 says, *"For the man who does not love his wife but divorces her, says the LORD, the God of Israel, covers his garment with violence, says the LORD of hosts. So guard*

yourselves in your spirit, and do not be faithless." Often the reason for divorce is that someone or both individuals have "fallen out of love." This passage makes it clear that "falling out of love" is not a valid excuse and the passage warns of violence and even challenges one's faith.

Romans 7

The third passage that is discussed in this topic comes from Romans 7:2-3, *"For a married woman is bound by law to her husband while he lives, but if her husband dies she is released from the law of marriage. Accordingly, she will be called an adulteress if she lives with another man while her husband is alive. But if her husband dies, she is free from that law, and if she marries another man she is not an adulteress."* The primary topic is not about divorce but whether someone can remarry after their partner dies. Scripture permits this, yet takes time to again say that couples should not get a divorce.

I am a victim of divorce, now what?

A divorce occurs and people are left in disarray. It can be the spouse, the children, a close friend, and even an in-law. Here are some helpful steps.

1. Remember God loves you.

John 3:16 says, *"For God so loved the world, that he gave his only Son, that whoever believes in him should not perish but have eternal life."* Augustine said, "God loves each of us as if there were only one of us."

2. Realize God hasn't forgotten you.

You may feel all alone. Joseph's story is written in the book of Genesis. He can relate. He was thrown in a pit fearing death, sold into slavery, falsely accused, locked-up in prison, and apparently forgotten, but God had a plan. God raised him to a position of influence and used him to save His people.

3. Be comforted in the fact that God has a plan.

You do not need to fear the future. Jeremiah 29:11 says, ***"For I know the plans I have for you, declares the LORD, plans for welfare and not for evil, to give you a future and a hope."***

4. Seek and give forgiveness – do right.

We can not control others, but we can and should control our own actions. It is always good to evaluate if you did anything wrong. If may not be as bad as someone else, but you know it was wrong. Then confess your sin to God and ask forgiveness from the other person. Next, it is time to forgive the other person. This does not mean you approve or condone their actions. It is not easy, but it is time to forgive them and not use it against them any more.

5. Pray.

Talking with God and taking time to listen to Him always needs to be a priority. Seek His presence. Enjoy His fellowship. Praise Him, thank Him, confess sin, and bring requests to Him. Look for Him to be active in your life and give Him credit for the blessings.

6. Read the Word.

Daily take time to see what God is saying in the Bible. Hebrews 4:12 says, *"For the word of God is living and active, sharper than any two-edged sword, piercing to the division of soul and of spirit, of joints and of marrow, and discerning the thoughts and intentions of the heart."* God's Word is alive and applicable to today's challenges.

7. Go to Church.

Get involved in a Christ-centered, Bible-believing Church. Go there to be comforted, but also go to encourage others. Hearing the Word, praising God with others, and being in a positive atmosphere is necessary.

8. Get involved in a growth community.

A growth community is more than just a Bible study. Obviously Bible study is important, but we also need to share our lives. We can learn from others' experiences and they can learn from ours.

9. Press on.

Paul says in Philippians 3:13, 14, *"Brothers, I do not consider that I have made it my own. But one thing I do: forgetting what lies behind and straining forward to what lies ahead, I press on toward the goal for the prize of the upward call of God in Christ Jesus."* You need to focus on the future. Do not let the past hold you back. Press on for what God has for you.

10. Look for others to help.

Sometimes the best therapy is to take the focus off our own problems and focus on others. 2 Corinthians 1:3-4 says, ***"Blessed be the God and Father of our Lord Jesus Christ, the Father of mercies and God of all comfort, who comforts us in all our affliction, so that we may be able to comfort those who are in any affliction, with the comfort with which we ourselves are comforted by God."*** God will comfort you. You can and should use your experiences to comfort others.

Marriage was designed by God. It is a gift from Him. He takes it seriously. Hebrews 13:4 says, ***"Let marriage be held in honor among all, and let the marriage bed be undefiled, for God will judge the sexually immoral and adulterous."***

> I take you for my lawful spouse,
> to have and to hold from this day forward,
> for better, for worse,
> for richer, for poorer,
> in sickness and health,
> until death do us part.

FAMILY WORKSHOP

APPENDIX 2

WORKSHOP NOTES

FAMILY WORKSHOP

SESSION 1

MONEY

John Carter | Director of Finance & HR

Matthew 6:19-24
What verse do you see being the main point of this passage? _____ (hint it's in the middle.)

What does this passage teach us to treasure?
_____

Can your heart Treasure God and Money at the same time?
_____

Question to ponder...What are the treasures your heart is focused on? Write a few down...
1.
2.
3.
4.

Matthew 6:25-34
How does this passage prioritize the needs that money deals with (verse 33)?

Does worrying help us in any way (verse 27)?

How are you compared to the birds of the air?

How is Solomon compared to the Lilly in the field?

What comfort can this give us?

Question to ponder? What are some of your worries you have right now? Are they needs or are they wants? Write them down, and give them to God.

It is important to have the proper perspective when dealing with finances. The above section is where we should all start to focus our hearts on God before we focus on ourselves. We serve an awesome God, and he knows what we are going through in life and he will ensure that our basic need are taken care of. Does that mean then, that we do not have to pay are bills? Should we not have a care to use discernment or wisdom with our finances? Let's see what else the bible says about finances... and some practical truth about wealth and money.

<u>Proverbs 13</u>
This chapter in Proverbs has many wise sayings and deals with the subject of how to heed or follow wise instructions. (I would encourage you to read the entire chapter) When dealing with money issues it is never a bad idea to seek wise council, in fact I would say it is always a good idea to seek wisdom.
What does verse 4 deal with?
What are the two contracting perspectives in this passage?

What does verse 7 & 8 deal with?
How does perspective play a role in this passage?

What does verse 11 deal with?

What is the practical way to build up savings?

Have you ever heard what happens to the lotto winners?

Hebrews 13:5-6
What does it mean to be free from the love of Money?

What does it mean to be content with what you have?

Ecclesiastes 5:10-19
What does this passage teach us about the love of money?

What truth does verse 15 give us?

What is the good truth that Solomon is trying to teach in verses 18 & 19?

What does it mean to accept his lot and rejoice in his toil?

I Timothy 6:6-10
What is the instruction given in verse 6-9?

What is the caution given to those who crave money in verses 9-10?

Have you ever heard the expression, "Live within your means?"

How does being content apply to this phrase?

1 Timothy 6:17-19

What is the instruction given to the wealthy in these verses?
1. Do NOT be _____
2. Do NOT put hope in _____
3. But DO put your hope in _____
4. Who does the providing _____
5. What is the intention of the things that God gives us _____
6. We are to do _____, to be rich in _____
7. Be _____ and ready to _____
8. Thus storing up _____ as a good _____
9. Take hold of that which is truly life

Summary:
As one can see the Bible does not shy away from the subject of money. In fact, there is much to warn us about how money can cloud our sense of security. When we start to put our hope and trust in money and wealth we soon realize that our hearts are focused on the wrong thing. We need to keep God in the front of our money making decisions. Wise council is always a good idea when it comes to money matters. Who do you talk to when it comes to financial council? We cannot just ignore our current responsibilities and spend money with no regard. Wisdom and discretion play a huge part in how we are to spend the money entrusted to each individual. This looks different for each person and family. God has determined that some will be rich and some will be poor, both scenarios have their pros and cons. To the rich it is easy to forget where the security and hope of life comes from. To the poor it is an anxious thing to have to determine where ones next meal is coming from. The bible gives instructions and cautions for both the rich and the poor. Not to put the power and desire for wealth above the power and desire of God. Wealth and riches, no matter what state you are in, rich or poor, should never cloud your heart with anxiety or hopelessness because our hope is not in the current wealth we have or don't have...our hope is in Christ. As Matthew 6 summarizes, our heavenly Father feeds the birds and covers the field, how much more than do you think he is aware of our needs.

I. Money starts with the heart! – It begins with knowing who has the power to give and who has the power to take away.

II. Being content is a major aspect of wise financial decision making.

III. Hope in God does not negate our responsibilities or debts.

FAMILY WORKSHOP

SESSION 2

INTIMACY IN MARRIAGE

Pastor Trevor Cole | Operations Pastor

1. Talk

    a. Make _____ clear
    b. Share what _____

2. Practice

    a. Make _____
    b. Put the _____

3. Laugh

    a. Feel free to _____
    b. Don't take _____

4. Serve

    a. Marriage itself is a decision to _____
    b. Be _____ not _____

FAMILY WORKSHOP

SESSION 3

CONFLICT RESOLUTION

Pastor Caleb Combs | Gathering Pastor

Working Through Conflict

Ephesians 4:26-27 - *"Be angry and do not sin; do not let the sun go down on your anger, and give no opportunity to the devil."*

Matthew 18 is a Biblical must for dealing with conflict.

Step #1

Step #2

Step #3 _____

_____

_____

Are you a Peacemaker or Peacebreaker?

Found in the Peacemaker by Ken Sande

_____
_____
_____
_____

Matthew 5:9 - *"Blessed are the peacemakers, for they shall be called sons of God."*

Forgiveness or Bitterness ?

_____
_____
_____
_____

Forgiveness is not a decision but a PROCESS.

FAMILY WORKSHOP

FAMILY WORKSHOP

SESSION 4

GRAND PARENTING

Carole Combs | Wife of Lead Pastor Jim Combs

Be the grandest parent

1. Leave a legacy of faith 2 Timothy 1:5

2. Leave a legacy of love 1 Corinthians 13:1-8

3. Leave a legacy of wisdom 1 Corinthians 13:11-13

4. Leave a legacy of respect Romans 12:1-5

Parenting Adult Children

From God in the first place, a heart of dedication
1 Samuel 1:21-28

Love unconditionally, God loves your child more than you could ever love them

A progression from leading/teaching to influence, be an example

FAMILY WORKSHOP

SESSION 5

RAISING TEENS

Pastor Jayson Combs | Family Pastor

"Fathers, do not provoke your children to anger, but bring them up in the discipline and instruction of the Lord." Ephesians 6:4

1. This is a _____ thing:

    a. Living as an _____:

    b. Praying for a _____:

2. Discipline is about _____, and _____

    a. Fight to _____

    b. Learn to _____

3. Instruction is all about what you _____

    a. Use the _____

    b. Use your _____

FAMILY WORKSHOP

SESSION 6

ADDICTION IN THE FAMILY

Pastor Jim Combs | Pastor

From my loathing of an addict...

1 Corinthians 16:15
"Now I urge you, brothers—you know that the household of Stephanas were the first converts in Achaia, and that they have devoted themselves to the service of the saints." (ESV)

"I beseech you, brethren, (ye know the house of Stephanas, that it is the firstfruits of Achaia, and that they have addicted themselves to the ministry of the saints,)" (KJV)

1. Culture of Addictions

2. Characteristic of an Addiction

3. Conquering Addictions

...To my loving of an addict

FAMILY WORKSHOP

SESSION 7

THE 7 C'S OF PARENTING PRESCHOOLERS

Pastor Josh Combs | Lead Pastor

1. _____
Romans 3:23; Romans 5:8; Romans 6:23; Romans 10:9; 1 Corinthians 10:31

2. _____
Hebrews 13:8; 1 Corinthians 15:58; Galatians 6:9

3. _____
Ephesians 4:32

4. _____
Ephesians 6:4; Deuteronomy 6:7; Judges 2:10; Deuteronomy 11:19

5. _____
Proverbs 13:24; Hebrews 12:5-11; Proverbs 3:11-12; Proverbs 22:15

6. _____
Philippians 4:13; Joshua 1:9

7. _____
Genesis 35:16-19; Proverbs 22:6

FAMILY WORKSHOP

SESSION 8

VENUS, MARS, AND MY KIDS ARE CHASING PLUTO

Dr. Randy T. Johnson | Growth Pastor

Personality

Outgoing or Reserved

Task oriented or People oriented

DiSC	Influencer	Dominance	Cautiousness	Supportiveness
LaHaye	Sanguine			Phlegmatic
Work Style	Way	Way	Way	Way
Bible Representative				
Ideal Ministry	Speaker	Helps	Mercy	Teacher
Animal				
Specialty				
Fears				
Views Money				
Recover from Conflict				
RX: Your Perscription	Be stimulating and recognize them	Be direct and to the point	Be accurate	Be sincere and appreciate them

Love Languages

L-Tank (Love Tank)

L

T

A

N

K

Words of Affirmation
Words matter. This person treasures hearing, "I love you." Honest compliments and praise mean a great deal, and insults or harsh words are taken to heart.

Acts of Service
Doing household chores or helping out in the home office is, to this person, the equivalent of saying, "I adore you."

Receiving and Giving Gifts
From trinkets and flowers to diamond rings and season tickets, this person feels loved when you present them with a token of your affection.

Quality Time
This person wants your undivided attention. The gift of your time is worth more than any material present you could give.

Physical Touch
A gentle hand on the shoulder, a peck on the check, a warm embrace or simply sitting beside this person makes them feel loved.

FAMILY WORKSHOP

SESSION 9

BLENDED TO MENDED
Debbie Kerr | Office Administrator

1. **Step Up:** Discover a redemptive God who loves, forgives, restores and provides strength.

2. **Step Down**: Be willing to adjust expectations

3. **Two Step:** Marriage must be top priority

4. **Step in Line:**
    a) Co-Parenting
    b) Parent & Step-Parent Roles
    c) Unique Parenting Roles & Issues

Resource: *The Smart Stepfamily - 7 Steps to a happy family* by: Ron Deal

FAMILY WORKSHOP

SESSION 10

SHEPHERDING OUR KIDS
Pastor Chuck Lindsey | Reach Pastor

HIT THE TARGET – Heart not head

DOING BATTLE – The weapon of prayer

OUT IN FRONT – Leading by example

TOOLS – Age appropriate tools & methods

Q&A

FAMILY WORKSHOP

SESSION 11

EFFECTIVE DISCIPLINE IN A DEFECTIVE WORLD
Roy Townsend | Principal at Oakland Christian School

"Train children in the right way, and when old, they will not stray." Proverbs 22:6

We must equip our darling offspring to make the move from total dependence on us to independence, from being controlled by us to controlling themselves. (Where is the dependence on God?)

In childhood, well-meaning parents always made decisions for them. We must understand that making good choices is like any other activity: It has to be learned. (Do you play an instrument for them? Do you make their free-throws? Do you read for them?) (This is a performance-based thing)

I. Ineffective Parenting Styles
    a. _____Parents:
    b. _____Helicopter Model
    c. _____ Sergeant Parents
    d. Laissez-Faire Parent (_____)

II. The Effective Parenting Style
    a. The _____Parent

Questions:
Which parenting type did you grow up under?

Which parenting type would you most likely revert to in a difficult situation?

Which parenting type do you think our heavenly Father uses?

Skill Reminders

1. Affordable Versus Unaffordable Mistake: The road to wisdom is paved with mistakes…consequences…and our empathy.

2. The Power Of Empathy: The most successful parents used about the same consequences…but they used them with empathy instead of anger, frustration, or sarcasm.

   a. The most effective parents seemed to understand the importance of displaying love and understanding before holding their children accountable for their actions.

       i.   This is so sad;
      ii.   What a bummer;
     iii.   How sad;
     iv.   Oh, Man;
      v.   Dang;
     vi.   This stinks
    vii.   That's never good

   b. Empathy allows your child's poor decision to remain the "bad guy" while allowing you to remain the "good guy."

FAMILY WORKSHOP

FAMILY WORKSHOP

SESSION 12

SINGLE PARENTING

Mike and Kim Vallance | Greeting Team at The River Goodrich

My Story

You are not alone

Choose Joy

Discipline

Spiritual Leader

There is Hope

OUR MISSION

Matthew 28:19-20: *"Go therefore and make disciples of all nations, baptizing them in the name of the Father and of the Son and of the Holy Spirit, teaching them to observe all that I have commanded you. And behold, I am with you always, to the end of the age."*

REACH

At The River Church, you will often hear the phrase, "we don't go to church, we are the Church." We believe that as God's people, our primary purpose and goal is to go out and make disciples of Jesus Christ. We encourage you to reach the world in your local communities.

GATHER

Weekend Gatherings at The River Church are all about Jesus, through singing, giving, serving, baptizing, taking the Lord's Supper, and participating in messages that are all about Jesus and bringing glory to Him. We know that when followers of Christ gather together in unity, it's not only a refresher it's bringing life-change.

GROW

Our Growth Communities are designed to mirror the early church in Acts as having "all things in common." They are smaller collections of believers who spend time together studying the word, knowing and caring for one another relationally, and learning to increase their commitment to Christ by holding one another accountable.

The River Church
8393 E. Holly Rd. Holly, MI 48442
theriverchurch.cc • info@theriverchurch.cc

BOOKS BY THE RIVER CHURCH

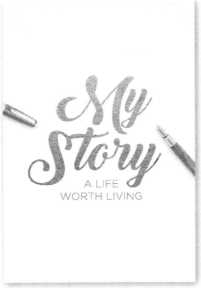

Made in the USA
San Bernardino, CA
15 January 2017